MW00640073

AN IDEAS INTO ACTION GUIDEBOOK

Choosing an Executive Coach

IDEAS INTO ACTION GUIDEBOOKS

Aimed at managers and executives who are concerned with their own and others' development, each guidebook in this series gives specific advice on how to complete a developmental task or solve a leadership problem.

LEAD CONTRIBUTORS	Karen Kirkland Miller
	Wayne Hart
GUIDEBOOK ADVISORY GROUP	Victoria A. Guthrie
	Cynthia D. McCauley
	Russ S. Moxley
DIRECTOR OF PUBLICATIONS	Martin Wilcox
EDITOR	Peter Scisco
WRITER	Janet Fox
DESIGN AND LAYOUT	Joanne Ferguson
CONTRIBUTING ARTIST	Laura J. Gibson

CCL No. 410
ISBN No. 1-882197-63-1

CENTER FOR CREATIVE LEADERSHIP
POST OFFICE BOX 26300
GREENSBORO, NORTH CAROLINA 27438-6300
336-288-7210

AN IDEAS INTO ACTION GUIDEBOOK

Choosing an Executive Coach

Karen Kirkland Miller and Wayne Hart

Center for ®
Creative Leadership

leadership. learning. life.

THE IDEAS INTO ACTION GUIDEBOOK SERIES

This series of guidebooks draws on the practical knowledge that the Center for Creative Leadership (CCL) has generated in the course of more than thirty years of research and educational activity conducted in partnership with hundreds of thousands of managers and executives. Much of this knowledge is shared – in a way that is distinct from the typical university department, professional association, or consultancy. CCL is not simply a collection of individual experts, although the individual credentials of its staff are impressive; rather it is a community, with its members holding certain principles in common and working together to understand and generate practical responses to today's leadership and organizational challenges.

The purpose of the series is to provide managers with specific advice on how to complete a developmental task or solve a leadership challenge. In doing that the series carries out CCL's mission to advance the understanding, practice, and development of leadership for the benefit of society worldwide. We think you will find the Ideas Into Action Guidebooks an important addition to your leadership toolkit.

Other guidebooks currently available:

- *Ongoing Feedback: How to Get It, How to Use It*
- *Becoming a More Versatile Learner*
- *Reaching Your Development Goals*
- *Giving Feedback to Subordinates*
- *Three Keys to Development: Defining and Meeting Your Leadership Challenges*
- *Feedback That Works: How to Build and Deliver Your Message*
- *Communicating Across Cultures*
- *Learning from Life: Turning Life's Lessons into Leadership Experience*
- *Keeping Your Career on Track: Twenty Success Strategies*
- *Preparing for Development: Making the Most of Formal Leadership Programs*

Table of Contents

EXECUTIVE BRIEF

Leadership in the top management ranks is often a lonely business. It can be difficult to get accurate feedback, for example, and it gets more difficult the higher you move in an organization. Many managers are reluctant to "open up" to colleagues, and sometimes it may be ill advised to do so. Yet it's difficult to improve leadership skills and job performance without input from others about strengths, weaknesses, and options for improvement. Many managers recognize that to focus their personal development plans they need the uninterrupted time and attention of a skilled, objective facilitator. This guidebook is for managers who are considering executive coaching as a tool in their personal leadership development. It describes what executive coaching is, and can help you decide whether coaching is appropriate for your situation. You'll also learn how to locate and select a qualified coach with the professional and personal credentials and characteristics that match your developmental needs so that you can achieve the goals you've set.

What Is Executive Coaching?

Executive coaching is a formal engagement in which a qualified coach works with an organizational leader in a series of dynamic, confidential sessions designed to establish and achieve clear goals that will result in improved business effectiveness, both for the individual and the organization. A good coach helps executives develop clarity of purpose and focus on action.

Coaching is not business consulting, organizational intervention, or psychological counseling. Coaching is different from a long-term mentoring relationship with a trusted colleague. These are all valuable interactions, but they require different skills from what a coach provides.

Executive coaching works best when it's part of a well-thought-out development plan. You might, for example, have a clear idea of the career path you desire, arrange a series of developmental assignments, get periodic 360-degree-survey feedback from co-workers, attend skills development classes, and schedule regular developmental discussions with your boss. In the context of such a development plan, coaching might specifically aim toward helping you achieve visible and measurable improvement in leadership effectiveness. Coaching is less powerful when it's undertaken in isolation from other developmental tools.

Does Executive Coaching Meet Your Needs?

Before you start looking for a coach, it's important to determine whether coaching is the best solution for you. Most managers can easily think of areas in which they could benefit from some expert help or advice, but executive coaches are not qualified to provide all the answers. To decide whether you want a coach or some other kind of counselor, consultant, or confidant, consider these statements:

not clear about technical issue

I need expert consulting services to help me solve a complicated business problem.

YES   Don't hire a coach. Instead, hire a business consultant.

NO   Continue ➤

may present as personal - but bus. implication

I need to discuss a deeply personal matter about my sense of well-being.

YES   Don't hire a coach. Instead, locate a licensed psychologist, psychiatrist, or counselor.

NO   Continue ➤

I need to discuss the internal politics of my organization and how it affects my career path.

YES   Don't hire a coach. Instead, find a trusted person within your organization who is willing to serve as a mentor.

NO   Continue ➤

All These

I need to learn and practice specific new skills that I lack.

YES Don't hire a coach. Instead, find an appropriate skill development course that offers many opportunities to practice the new skills, perhaps using videotaped feedback.

NO Continue ➤

I need to acquire a specific type of knowledge.

YES Don't hire a coach. Instead, consider your own learning style, and purchase the information in the form of books, tapes, or classes. Set aside time to study and internalize the information.

NO Continue ➤

I need to evaluate whether I am in the right career and explore options for changing my career or profession.

YES Don't hire a coach. Instead, hire an expert in career counseling who can administer aptitude and interest testing and who will assist you in this transition.

NO Continue ➤

I need structured planning and support to help in the accomplishment of a new way of leading or managing others.

YES Hire a coach.

What Developmental Challenges Are Suited to Coaching?

As you can see, there are some situations for which other kinds of consultants and counselors are more appropriate than a coach. Here are some examples of situations in which coaching can facilitate personal development.

Consider hiring a coach if:

- you've just completed a development program and have a heightened awareness of skills you need to develop or skills you may rely on too much
- you're faced with a significant increase in the scope of your responsibility
- you've taken on an unfamiliar assignment, such as leading a business turnaround, a start-up venture, a workforce reduction, or a rapid-growth situation
- you're a project manager who needs to develop better team-building skills
- you're a leader who wants to be successful at managing across geographic, cultural, or demographic boundaries
- you're a traditional manager who wants to move to a less dominant and directive leadership style
- you're an executive who needs to develop, articulate, and sell a new vision for your organization
- you're a line manager who wants to broaden your experience and capacity to take on an executive position
- you need a confidential sounding board to help you work out turning strategies into action
- you're a task-oriented manager who wants to develop interpersonal skills
- you're a technical manager who needs to become adept at articulating ideas, influencing others, and understanding organizational politics.

Coaching versus Counseling

Some managers are reluctant to engage an executive coach because they equate coaching with psychological counseling or psychiatry. They don't want someone probing into their childhood issues, diagnosing what's wrong with them, and attempting to "fix" them.

Executive coaching doesn't fit that medical model. There isn't an assumption of pathology – no belief that the manager being coached is psychologically deficient or needs to be cured. Executive coaches typically don't assume that the roots of management behavior can be or should be traced to events in the distant past.

As a rule, executive coaches don't ask why you are the way you are. They focus on how you can make the specific behavioral changes you want to make in line with your current values and goals. Coaches don't think in terms of what's wrong with you. They work to help you identify developmental needs, leverage your strengths, and become more effective in your work.

What to Expect from Executive Coaching

Coaching engagements typically last for six to eighteen months. The process usually begins with one or more face-to-face meetings in which you will build the necessary rapport and establish realistic guidelines and expectations. During the initial assessment period your coach will get to know you, not only by talking with you but (always with your permission and consent) through some combination of:

- questionnaires and psychological testing instruments that you fill out either on paper or online

CCL model

- interviews with your colleagues
- unobtrusive observation as you go about your work
- interviews with your customers
- interviews with your family members
- review of your performance appraisals.

The coaching sessions will include a review of your assessment information, setting goals, planning change strategies, monitoring and measuring progress against your goals, discussing any setbacks and obstacles that crop up, and celebrating your successes.

A coach may conduct sessions in person, by phone, by e-mail, or by videoconferencing. You and your coach can determine the frequency, length, and medium that suits your needs and your schedule.

Coaching sessions typically cost $300 per hour. A full package, including assessment, interviews, and a specified number of sessions, can cost between $10,000 and $30,000. A top-executive intervention with a pair of coaches can cost $75,000. In many cases, the cost of coaching is borne by the employer.

Feel Better or Work Better?

You shouldn't expect a money-back guarantee from a coach, but you should expect to see some improvement in your leadership skills within six months. The purpose of coaching is not to make you feel better about yourself, though it often does. The purpose is to change the way you operate in ways that are measurable and observable by yourself and others.

Therefore, you should set some specific goals with your coach at the outset of the engagement. Discuss with your coach how progress toward these goals will be measured. Pencil-and-paper surveys usually are not sufficient to measure behavioral change, so some interview-based methods may need to be used.

Evaluating an Executive Coach

Locating the right coach is like finding the right person to fill a key position in your organization. You may want to check out several candidates before you make your selection. You can do initial screening by phone and e-mail. Some questions for this stage are:

- What training in coaching have you received?
- Have you coached individuals in my industry?
- What companies have you worked with?
- How will you assess my current skills?
- What is your philosophy of coaching?
- How will you measure improvement?
- How long do you anticipate the coaching engagement will last?

If you're at the chief executive level, you might also ask how many CEOs the individual has worked with as a coach.

Preliminary screening will help you narrow the search to a short list of coaches who have the competence and experience you're looking for. Watch out for individuals who give vague answers to your questions or try to snow you with a slick sales pitch. Be wary of those who anticipate that the coaching engagement will extend beyond eighteen months – that may indicate an ineffective coaching style or strategy. After you have identified a few good prospects you can conduct interviews.

Competence, Chemistry, and Trust

For coaching to deliver on its promise, it's important to find the coach who is right for you. You need a coach who has business and organizational knowledge along with excellent interpersonal skills. Equally important, you need a coach with whom you feel comfortable.

Finding the right coach can be a tall order because executive coaching is an unlicensed profession. As it stands now, anyone can open a coaching business. It's up to you to ask the questions to determine whether the individual has the appropriate experience and skills.

You may have a strong preference for someone of your own gender or someone of your generation. You may find it more stimulating and productive to work with someone who is different from you. Only you can determine whether the coach you're considering encourages your trust and confidence. Honor your personal values. If a potential coach strikes you as too slick, too frivolous, too formal, too talkative, too judgmental – trust your intuition. Coaching benefits you only if your coach is someone you respect, someone who puts you at ease.

Safety and trust are paramount in coaching engagements. While you may do business with people you can't rely on absolutely to keep confidences and not exploit private information, your coach must be totally reliable in this regard. Coaching won't work if you don't feel completely safe about revealing your doubts, frustrations, and feelings about yourself, your colleagues, and your organization.

When you've identified a prospective coach whom you believe is trustworthy, make sure he or she understands how the relationship needs to be structured to assure your comfort. Here are some suggestions:

- Schedule your coaching sessions away from your business location.
- If you agree to have your coach observe you at work, decide in advance how he or she will be introduced to others in your office.

handling info offered unsolicited by observers -

- If other people – your associates, customers, or family members – are to be involved in the initial assessment, you should stipulate whether some topics are "off limits."
- Be sure there is a written contract specifying the confidentiality agreement.
- Inquire about the coach's practice of keeping notes and records, and get assurance as to the security of those records.
- Decide if you're willing to let your coach use you as a reference and stipulate how you want that handled.

The highest levels of safety and comfort tend to occur in coaching relationships that are purely developmental, not evaluative. It may be desirable, however, for others to be involved in assisting you in reaching goals, measuring change, encouraging opportunities for you to practice new behaviors, and rewarding progress. Be sure there is a written agreement to secure your consent to involve any other people in the coaching engagement.

Interviewing the Prospective Coach

You should expect to pay for the initial face-to-face meeting with a prospective coach. Let the individual know that you haven't made up your mind yet but that you want some time to assess whether the two of you would be able to work well together. Your prospective coach should make the same determination.

During the interview it's better to ask open-ended questions rather than questions that encourage a simple "Yes" or "No." You want to get a feel for the person's values, character, and interpersonal style, as well as get answers to any questions you have about professional credentials and experience.

Watch and listen carefully to how the prospective coach responds. Pay attention to how he or she makes you feel. The purpose of coaching is to help you change your behavior. Changing behavior is always hard work and almost always involves temporary discomfort, awkwardness, and the temptation to revert to familiar patterns and habits. You need to have confidence that your coach is someone who can support you, motivate you, and hold you accountable through personal change in a manner that is both honest and respectful of your dignity. You need to feel that your coach is both skillful and compassionate.

In your first meeting with a candidate for coach, look for these qualities:

- *Executive presence.* The coach should immediately impress you as polished, professional, and articulate. The coach should inspire confidence by his or her own self-confidence and ease.

- *Strong interpersonal skills.* The coach should be a good listener, able to pick up on what you say and to discern the thoughts and feelings behind your words. Is your prospective coach able to confront and challenge statements with which he or she disagrees? Is the coach straightforward in manner, not afraid to ask for clarification? Does the coach have a sense of humor, and does that sense of humor appeal to you? Does the coach strike you as a warm and empathetic person? Does the coach seem to be using your conversation to build rapport and trust, or simply to get hired?

- *Ability to be credible and authentic as a person.* Are you getting a sense that the coach is genuine and straightforward, or that the coach is trying to give the "right" answers? Does your prospective coach seem to be "going through the motions" or is there something more concrete and real in the responses to your questions?

- *Skill and knowledge in the use of formal assessment tools.* What kinds of psychological tests will the coach use? Why are those particular tests appropriate for you? What kind of training has the coach had in interpreting test results? How does the coach combine and synthesize data from multiple sources? How will the coach use the assessment data in the ongoing engagement?
- *Maturity.* Regardless of the coach's age, he or she should possess the self-awareness and stability to be a good role model. Signs of emotional maturity include willingness to keep learning, the ability to tolerate stress and handle crises, good impulse control, the ability to live with ambiguity and uncertainty, and comfort in receiving feedback.
- *Strong ethical sense.* Your coach should be sensitive to confidentiality. If your prospective coach brags about other clients or gossips about the inner workings of other companies, you can read that as having little respect for confidentiality. Your coach should also exhibit honesty and integrity, and be strong enough to tell you the truth even when you'd rather not hear it.
- *Flexibility.* Good coaches have the ability to work well with the whole range of personality types and to shift gears when a particular approach is ineffective. Your coach should also have the flexibility to work within the constraints of your schedule. That might mean, for example, that you combine phone conversations or e-mail messages when you are traveling with longer face-to-face sessions.
- *Solid knowledge of learning theories and change-process dynamics.* Coaching sessions aren't just informal conversations. The expert coach keeps an eye on the goal, pacing and guiding the sessions to bring about the desired learning

and behavioral changes. More than a cheerleader or a sympathetic ear, the coach must be someone who understands how adults learn and grow and must have the skills to facilitate that learning.

- *Ability to plan, implement, and manage a relationship over time.* You've probably encountered people who make a brilliant first impression but whose subsequent performance is disappointing. You want to make sure that the coach not only interviews well but can manage a relationship over

---

Business Expert or Psychologist?

In reading over the characteristics of a good coach you may have realized that the best coaches combine business experience and psychological counseling skills. Both are necessary. You would have trouble discussing your work situation and your organizational challenges with a coach who didn't have current knowledge of business issues and organizational dynamics. On the other hand, you could not get the guidance and support you need to change your behavior from a business colleague who lacked training in psychological assessment and behavioral counseling.

Some coaches are psychologists by education and background. Others come out of the ranks of business executives and consultants. Whatever the educational background, coaches need continuing education in both business and behavioral science.

As part of your screening of prospective coaches, ask what they do to deepen and update both the business and psychological skills they bring to the coaching process.

time. Ask about the process and progress of past coaching engagements – no names, of course – to judge how the coach moves his or her client toward specific goals over the course of a long-term coaching engagement.

- *A positive focus.* The starting point of your coaching engagement should be the strengths and skills you bring to your leadership position. Coaching works best when it's built on leveraging strengths rather than on fixing deficiencies. Your intelligence, abilities, and resourcefulness are the primary sources of your capacity for growth and change. Look for signs that the prospective coach recognizes and respects your strengths and has the confidence that they will carry you through the challenges of making the changes that will make you a more effective leader.

Where to Find a Coach

Finding an executive coach who is qualified to provide what you want can be difficult because coaching is an unregulated field of practice. There are no licensing boards, certification requirements, or impartial consortiums that rate providers of coaching services. Here are some sources for locating executive coaches:

- The human resources department of your company may be able to refer you to a coach.
- Management consulting and training firms frequently provide executive coaching services. Check directories on the World Wide Web, such as Yahoo's management

consulting index, or consult your human resources department for help in locating and evaluating such firms.

- In addition to directories of consulting firms, the Web contains many specific coaching sites. You'll have to do your homework to verify that they are reliable and have a track record of success. One place to start is the Professional Coaches and Mentors Association at *www.pcmaonline.com*.

- Word of mouth is as valuable in finding executive coaches as it is for identifying other professional services. Friends and associates may be able to recommend a coach.

These sources are just a starting point. Once you have a name you will still need to proceed carefully. It will be up to you to ask for references and to ascertain the individual's education, training, business experience, ethical guidelines, confidentiality practices, fees, engagement duration, and continuing education. And even a coach who passes the qualifications test with flying colors may still not be the right coach for you. It's up to you to determine whether the chemistry is right.

Choosing Your Coach Checklist

You now have a sense of when coaching is a valuable developmental tool, what kind of time commitment is involved, what the fees are likely to be, and what the process of finding the right coach will entail. Is coaching right for you? Only you can decide.

❏ I am ready to make a commitment of time, money, and energy in my own development.

❏ I am interested in coaching services because I want to improve, not because someone else (my boss, my spouse, my colleague) wants me to change.

❏ I am capable of participating in a rigorously honest self-appraisal.

❏ I am humble enough to realize I'm not perfect and that another person can help me become more effective.

❏ I'm willing and able to devote the necessary time and effort to work with a coach over a period of several months.

❏ I'm capable of trusting another person enough to talk candidly about my weaknesses and mistakes.

❏ I'm confident that I have the ability to change my behavior.

Your honest responses to these statements will help you see if the time is right for you to work with a coach. If your responses indicate that you aren't a candidate for coaching, you shouldn't hire a coach. Coaching sessions would only be a waste of time for both of you.

If your responses reveal that you're ready, willing, and able, you've taken the first steps toward a successful coaching relationship. True, the coach you select must be qualified, experienced, and skillful. But you must uphold your side of the bargain too. A successful coaching engagement requires that you be open to change, ready for growth, and willing to invest your energy in learning to be a more effective leader.

Suggested Readings

Douglas, C. A., & Morley, W. H. (2000). *Executive coaching: An annotated bibliography*. Greensboro, NC: Center for Creative Leadership.

Dutton, G. (1997). Executive coaches call the plays. *Management Review, 86*(2), 39-45.

Eggers, J., & Clark, D. (2000). Executive coaching that wins. *Ivey Business Journal, 65*(1), 66-70.

Guthrie, V. A. (1999). *Coaching for action: A report on long-term advising in a program context*. Greensboro, NC: Center for Creative Leadership.

Judge, W., & Cowell, J. (1997). The brave new world of executive coaching. *Business Horizons, 40*(4), 71-77.

Kaplan, R. E. (1999). *Internalizing strengths: An overlooked way of overcoming weaknesses in managers*. Greensboro, NC: Center for Creative Leadership.

Thach, L., & Heinselman, T. (1999). Executive coaching defined. *Training & Development, 53*(3), 34-39.

Turner, F. (2000). Caveat emptor: The pitfalls of coaching. *Orlando Business Journal, 17*(8), 31.

Witherspoon, R., & White, R. P. (1997). *Four essential ways that coaching can help executives*. Greensboro, NC: Center for Creative Leadership.

Background

CCL's experience with executive coaching dates back more than ten years. During that time a coaching-and-support role called *process advisor* played a significant part in the developmental experiences of clients participating in CCL's Awareness Program for Executive Excellence (APEX)® and LeaderLab® programs. The process advisor works closely with individual participants to help them understand and develop goals in a professional relationship lasting from six months to one year.

CCL's executive-coaching process adheres to its respect for individuals and diversity, focuses on building on the leader's existing strengths, and provides a confidential, safe setting in which serious developmental work can be accomplished. Based on its long experience in working with such long-term coaching relationships, CCL has noted and agreed upon several best practices:

- a completely voluntary engagement for both the coach and client
- an explanation of what coaching is and is not
- the use and leverage of the client's abundant intelligence and talent
- fully informed consent regarding confidentiality or the terms of sharing of information with organizational stakeholders
- careful protection of assessment information, written records, and the client's identity
- a subjective feeling of safety to promote optimum learning
- a solution-focused approach
- an action-learning approach

- a focus on managing change and stimulating innovation
- clearly stated session limits and specific developmental goals
- a separation from corporate selection or promotion decisions
- a simple, focused approach that may be guided by a mix of assessment, challenge, and support strategies
- an option for easy termination at any time
- a firm grounding in CCL research and knowledge
- a firm grounding in current academic and applied knowledge in business and psychology
- an understanding that development is a life-long process
- an openness to the use of a wide variety of theories and tools
- an expectation of continuously evaluating and improving the coaching relationship
- the use of ongoing quality control procedures to ensure excellence.

The Center for Creative Leadership certifies, monitors, and provides continuing education for executive coaches, and maintains a global directory of coaches it has recruited and trained.

Key Point Summary

Executive coaching has become an increasingly popular option for managers and executives who need individualized, unbiased input to help them make the most of their developmental experiences. In its simplest terms, executive coaching is a formal engagement that matches a qualified coach with an organizational leader in a series of dynamic, confidential sessions designed to establish and achieve clear goals. A good coaching relationship improves business effectiveness for both the individual leader and the organization.

Coaching works best when it's part of a development plan. Managers and executives looking to capitalize on their developmental experiences should carefully consider whether coaching is the best solution for their particular leadership challenge and situation. Although most executives can think of areas in which they could benefit from expert help or advice, executive coaches can't provide all the answers.

Coaching engagements usually begin with one or more lengthy face-to-face meetings in which the coach and the client build the rapport necessary for honest communication and establish realistic guidelines and expectations. Preliminary screening helps to narrow the coaching search. Be wary of prospective coaches who give vague answers to questions or concentrate more on a sales pitch than on initial communication. Executives in the market for a coach should also keep in mind that eighteen months is really the longest span of time that a coaching engagement is likely to last – if the prospective coach says it will take longer, then it's fair to ask how effective a coach he or she really is.

For coaching to deliver its promised results, executives need to find the right coach. Finding the right coach can be a challenge because executive coaching is an unlicensed profession. Executives should look for a coach with whom they are comfortable, whom they trust, who has business and organizational knowledge, and who brings to the working relationship excellent interpersonal skills.

Managers who have identified skill areas they want to improve can often benefit dramatically from coaching. Coaches can and should be selected to mesh effectively with the manager's personality and preferred learning style. In addition, a leader seeking a coaching engagement should be open to change, ready for growth, and willing to invest energy and time in learning to be a more effective leader.

Order Form

To order, complete and return a copy of this form or contact the Center's Publication Area at: Post Office Box 26300 • Greensboro, NC 27438-6300 • Phone 336-545-2810 • Fax 336-282-3284. You can also order via the Center's online bookstore at www.ccl.org/publications

	QUANTITY	SUBTOTAL
❑ I would like to order additional copies of **Choosing an Executive Coach** (#410) $8.95 ea.*		
❑ I would like to order other Ideas Into Action Guidebooks.		
❑ **Ongoing Feedback** (#400) $8.95 ea.*		
❑ **Reaching Your Development Goals** (#401) $8.95 ea.*		
❑ **Becoming a More Versatile Learner** (#402) $8.95 ea.*		
❑ **Giving Feedback to Subordinates** (#403) $8.95 ea.*		
❑ **Three Keys to Development** (#404) $8.95 ea.*		
❑ **Feedback That Works** (#405) $8.95 ea.*		
❑ **Communicating Across Cultures** (#406) $8.95 ea.*		
❑ **Learning from Life** (#407) $8.95 ea.*		
❑ **Keeping Your Career on Track** (#408) $8.95 ea.*		
❑ **Preparing for Development** (#409) $8.95 ea.*		
❑ **Feedback Package** (#724; includes #400, #403, #405) $17.95 ea.		
Add sales tax if resident of CA (7.5%), CO (6%), NC (6%)	SALES TAX	
U.S. shipping and handling (add 6%, with a minimum of $4) Non-U.S. shipping and handling (add 40%, with an $8 minimum) Express shipping service available	SHIPPING	
CCL's Federal Tax ID #23-707-9591	TOTAL	

*Single title quantity discounts: 1-4 – $8.95; 5-99 – $7.95; 100-499 – $6.50; 500+ – $5.95

DISCOUNTS ARE AVAILABLE
IF ORDERING BY MAIL OR FAX, PLEASE COMPLETE INFORMATION BELOW.

PAYMENT

❑ My check or money order is enclosed. **(Prepayment required for orders less than $100.)**

❑ Charge my order, plus shipping, to my credit card.

❑ American Express   ❑ Discover   ❑ MasterCard   ❑ Visa

Acct. # _____   Expiration Date: Mo./Yr. _____

Signature _____

SHIP TO

Name _____

Title _____

Organization _____

Street Address _____

City/State/Zip _____

Phone ( ) _____
Your telephone number is required for shipping.

❑ **CHECK HERE TO RECEIVE A COMPLETE GUIDE TO CCL PUBLICATIONS.**
❑ **CHECK HERE TO RECEIVE INFORMATION ABOUT CCL PROGRAMS AND PRODUCTS.**

ORDER BY PHONE: 336-545-2810 • ONLINE: WWW.CCL.ORG/PUBLICATIONS